FIND OUT ABOUT
MAGNETS

With 15 projects and more than 200 pictures

STEVE PARKER

ARMADILLO

This edition is published by Armadillo, an imprint of Anness Publishing Ltd, Blaby Road, Wigston, Leicestershire LE18 4SE; info@anness.com; www.annesspublishing.com

If you like the images in this book and would like to investigate using them for publishing, promotions or advertising, please visit our website www.practicalpictures.com for more information.

Publisher: Joanna Lorenz
Editor: Sam Batra
Consultant: Alison Porter, BSc, Science Museum, London
Photographer: John Freeman
Stylists: Thomasina Smith and Isolde Sommerfeldt
Designer: Caroline Reeves
Picture Researcher: Liz Eddison
Illustrator: Kuo Kang Chen
Production Controller: Ben Worley

PICTURE CREDITS

Manufacturer: Anness Publishing Ltd, Blaby Road, Wigston, Leicestershire LE18 4SE, England
For Product Tracking go to: www.annesspublishing.com/tracking
Batch: 0352-21026-1127

PUBLISHER'S NOTE

CONTENTS

4 • Magnets and magnetism

6 • What is a magnet?

8 • Making magnets

10 • History of magnets

12 • What do magnets attract?

14 • Poles apart

16 • Seeing magnetism

18 • Push and pull

20 • Magnets and their uses

22 • Magnetic fishing

24 • The biggest magnet

26 • How a compass works

28 • The Magnetic Poles

30 • Magnets in space

32 • Magnets and maps

34 • Magnetic sense

36 • Electric magnets

38 • Making an electromagnet

40 • EM machines

42 • The EM Olympics

44 • Magnetism in motors

46 • Motorized machines

48 • Sound to magnetism

50 • Magnets as storage space

52 • Magnetism and sound

54 • Magnetic music

56 • Magnets and computers

58 • Magnetic *Formula 1*

60 • Magnets of the future

62 • Tricks with magnets

64 • Index

The publishers would like to thank the following children from St John the Baptist Church of England School and Walnut Tree Walk Primary School: Danny Bill, Katie Blue, Tony Borg, Stephen Grimshaw, Lauren Kendrick, Sharday Manahan, Mikki Melaku, Yew Hong Mo, Nickolas Moore, Louise Morgan, Lola Olayinka, Yemisi Omolewa, Stephen Reid, Gemma Turland, Joe Westbrook – and also Sophie and Alex Lindblom-Smith. Thanks also to Caroline Beattie, the Early Learning Centre, London and Broadhurst, and Clarkson and Fuller, London.

MAGNETS AND MAGNETISM

A magnet inside a vivid plastic case can hold pieces of paper on metal surfaces such as those of a refrigerator or washing machine. Enjoy rearranging them as often as you like.

Have you used a magnet today? Perhaps you fixed a message on the refrigerator door with a magnetic note-holder. Magnets and magnetism are found in many other places, too. Almost any device or machine that has an electric motor uses magnetism – from a CD or DVD player to a washing machine or dryer. Countless other pieces of equipment and machinery also use magnetism, in the home, school, office and factory. They include computers, radios, power drills, and even giant electricity-making power stations. Magnetism is still a mysterious force that cannot be seen. Yet we live with its effects every day.

Speed
Are there magnets on bicycles? Some bicycles have a speedometer that works with a spinning magnet. If the bicycle's lights are powered by a dynamo, that also uses magnetism.

A warm blow
The electric motor in a hair-dryer uses magnetism. It spins a small fan that blows warm air at you and dries your hair.

Finding the way
Today's boats and ships have satellite navigation systems. However, they still use a magnetic compass to check their route and find the way, just like sailors did hundreds of years ago.

Making music
To create its sound, the electric guitar relies on magnetism to make electrical signals. The guitar is plugged into an electric amplifier so that its sound can be heard.

Flying high
Modern aircraft have magnetic compasses and many of their dials, systems and equipment use magnetism. Magnets also let the pilots take a rest as they are used in the autopilot that controls the plane for part of the journey.

WHAT IS A MAGNET?

MAGNETS are usually made of the element called iron, or another metal that has lots of iron in it, such as steel. They can be various shapes, big or small, but all magnets have a special ability that seems almost magical. They can pull things towards themselves by an invisible force called magnetism. But a magnet only attracts, or pulls, certain things, mainly those that are made of iron, or contain iron.

A magnet's power to attract can be transferred through objects. To see this, attach a steel paper-clip to a magnet. Then, attach another paper-clip to the first and so on until you have made a chain.

Making magnet metal

Most magnets are made from iron, or from steel that contains iron. The raw materials come from ore or rocks with iron in them. These are heated until they melt.

Shape and size

You cannot identify magnets by their shape or size. They can be straight bars, buttons, horseshoes and many other shapes. They may be red, but that is just paint to make them look good. This is a horseshoe magnet. Magnets are often shaped like this.

Jumbled-up micro-magnets.

Lined-up micro-magnets.

Tiny magnets

Think of a bar of iron as having millions of micro-magnets inside it, called domains. If these are all jumbled up, the bar is not a magnet. If the micro-magnets in a bar are lined up and point the same way, it is a magnet.

Atoms

The tiny domains, or micro-magnets, inside iron are actually groups of atoms. All materials – metals, non-metals, gases and liquids – are made from atoms, and only the most powerful microscopes can see them. Atoms spin around and around, just like a ball balanced on the tip of your finger.

FACT BOX

• You cannot tell if something is a magnet simply by looking at its shape or size, or if it is black, blue, red or silver. You need to test it with objects that contain iron.

• Ordinary types of magnets are called permanent magnets. They are magnetic all the time, and they keep their magnetism for months and years. There are other kinds of magnets, such as electromagnets, whose strength and magnetism vary.

• A typical magnet has two poles, where the magnetic force is strongest.

• Most metals are not magnetic. The most common magnetic metals are cobalt, nickel and iron.

MAKING MAGNETS

Y OU can make your own magnet from a rod, strip or bar of something made of iron or steel that is not already a magnet. To do this, you also need a ready-made magnet. There are many suitable items made from steel, from screws to screwdrivers. Try some objects that are made from different metals, like brass or aluminium, or from other substances such as wood, plastic or paper. See what you discover when you experiment with these other materials, and then compare your conclusions with the findings made when iron or steel is used.

You will need: an iron nail, magnet, paper-clips, brass pin.

A simple horseshoe magnet is a familiar but fascinating object.

Your own magnet

Take an iron nail and stroke it about 50 times with one end of a ready-made magnet. Stroke it along its length from one end to the other. The nail is now a magnet itself. Can it pick up a paper-clip or a brass pin?

Movement of pole of horseshoe magnet

This diagram shows how to move the magnet when stroking the nail. Remember to always use the same pole, to move in the same direction and to lift the magnet clear after each stroke.

Does it stick?
Objects made of brass or other metals, apart from iron or steel, cannot usually be made into magnets. Do they even stick to a proper magnet?

Ruining a magnet
Use the iron nail that you have made into a magnet. Carefully tap it hard several times with the hammer. This shakes up all the tiny micro-magnets inside and destroys the magnetism.

You will need: brass screw, magnet, iron nail, hammer, empty aluminium drinks can, paper-clip.

Non-magnetic metal
The drinks can is aluminium. It does not stick to a ready-made magnet. You cannot make it into a magnet by stroking, either, no matter how long you might try!

Testing magnets
The usual test for a magnet is to try and pick up something made of iron or steel. If an iron nail is too heavy for a weak magnet, try a shiny steel paper-clip instead.

HISTORY OF MAGNETS

PEOPLE have known about magnets and magnetism for thousands of years. This is because some magnets occur naturally. In certain places, you can pick them up from the ground. These natural magnets usually come in the form of lumps of stone called lodestone or magnetite, a type of rock that contains lots of iron. Ancient peoples noticed that two lumps of this rock might try to stick together or push apart. Then sailors and explorers discovered how to use thin slivers of this rock as magnetic compasses to find their way. However, people have only understood more about magnets in the last 200 years.

A typical bar magnet has two ends called poles. The invisible magnetism, called lines of magnetic force, is strongest around these ends.

The compass
About 1,000 years ago, sailors and explorers made a discovery. They found that a thin piece of lodestone, floating freely in a bowl of water, would always point the same way – north and south. They had discovered the magnetic compass.

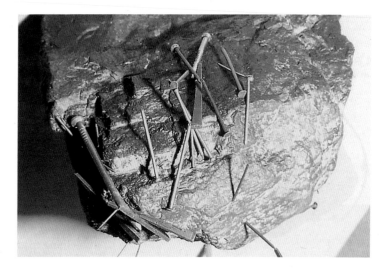

Magnetic rock
Lodestone, also called magnetite, is a natural magnet. When dug out of the ground, iron-containing objects such as nails and pins stick to it – just as they do to manufactured magnets.

Compass on board

During the great days of sailing ships, the magnetic compass was a vital piece of equipment. It showed which way was north, south, east or west. The navigator used the compass and maps to follow the ship's position.

Better compasses

In the 1600s, compasses were being made using strips of magnetized iron, which were allowed to twirl around freely. The compass was put in an elegant, portable box that was decorated with attractive designs and patterns.

The fabled land

Some adventurers suggested that the North Pole, to which a magnetic compass points, was a paradise bathed in sunlight and peace. Others wanted to discover new trade routes by finding a way around the top of North America, as a short cut to the East. But their ships got trapped, their camps froze and many explorers died. The Magnetic North Pole was first reached by British explorer James Ross and his expedition in 1831.

FACT BOX

• The name magnet may come from Magnesia. This was a region in Thessaly, in Ancient Greece. A part of modern Greece in the same area is called Magnisia.

• More than 2,500 years ago, the Ancient Greeks knew of the mysterious powers of the rock called lodestone.

• No one is sure who invented the first magnetic compass. It may have been the Ancient Chinese, about 1,800 years ago. By the year CE1000, the Chinese were using compasses to find their way at sea.

• By the 1100s, the use of compasses had spread as far as the Middle East and Europe.

WHAT DO MAGNETS ATTRACT?

M OST ordinary magnets attract only certain objects. These are things containing the metal iron. So, how can you tell if an object is made of iron or contains iron? Try testing it with a magnet. For some objects the attraction is very weak, so you have to do this carefully and feel for the pulling force. For other objects, the attraction is strong enough to make them stick to the magnet. Remember that it is the magnet that does the pulling and not the object, unless that is a magnet too!

The human body has tiny amounts of iron in the blood, but too little to be affected by a magnet.

Cans

A fizzy-drinks can is probably made of aluminium. This is a metal, but it is not iron. The magnet does not pull or attract it. You could try an empty food can, such as for baked beans or soup. What happens then?

M A T E R I A L S

You will need: magnet, aluminium drinks can, empty food can, plastic or glass beaker, stainless steel fork, book, paper, cardboard, paper-clip, metal washers and aluminium cooking foil.

WARNING
Be careful when testing sharp objects, such as needles, nails, pins and cans. Do not hang breakable objects on a magnet. A sudden jolt might make them fall to the floor!

Paper, card and board
Try the magnetic test on a book or a sheet of paper. Does the magnet attract them? Can the magnetism attract a paper-clip? Will it pass through the book or paper? Try different thicknesses of these materials and note down your results.

Glass and plastic
Try the beaker to see if the magnet attracts it. Glass and plastic do not contain iron, so they are not magnetic. See if the magnetism can pass through the beaker by holding the magnet on the outside and putting the fork on the inside.

Just passing through
Test metal washers with a magnet. They are probably steel, so they are attracted to it. Test cooking foil, too. It is probably aluminium, so it is not attracted. Now test the washers, with the foil between them and the magnet. Does the magnetism pass through the foil?

POLES APART

Some magnets, such as this bar magnet (left), have their different poles coded or marked. It is usually red or marked N for north. Blue, or sometimes silver, may represent S for south.

THE two poles, or ends, of a magnet may look the same, but they are not. Put one pole of a magnet near to a pole of another magnet to find out the differences. You may feel an attraction force, or pulling, as the two poles stick together strongly. Alternatively, you may feel a repulsion force, or pushing, as the two poles twist and repel each other. The different poles are called the north pole and the south pole. In all magnets two identical poles will push each other away, while two different poles will pull towards each other. These are basic features of all magnets.

Like poles repel
'Like poles repel, unlike poles attract.' This saying helps you to remember a vital feature about magnets. It means that poles that are the same will repel, or push each other apart. Put two north poles together, and they repel. Two south poles also repel.

Unlike poles attract

The poles of two magnets that are different, or opposite, will attract. Put a north pole and south pole together and they will attract.

North and south

Why are a magnet's poles called north and south? This is because the north pole points to the Magnetic North Pole in the Arctic at the top of the world. The south pole points to the Magnetic South Pole on Antarctica. Their full names are north-seeking pole and south-seeking pole.

Poles and shapes

Magnetism is concentrated around the poles of a magnet. In the button-shaped note-holder magnets *(above)*, each pole is on an opposite side of the button. This is why the magnet sticks to the fridge sideways-on.

Push-up train

Some trains have no wheels. Instead there are magnets in the base of the train and magnetism in the track. The like poles face each other, so they repel, lifting the train so it floats by magnetic repulsion. This is called magnetic levitation, or maglev.

SEEING MAGNETISM

Yᴏᴜ cannot see the magnetic force around a magnet. But you can see the effects of its presence when an iron nail sticks to a magnet. You can see the shape and extent of a magnetic field by using tiny, powder-like pieces of iron called iron filings. Magnetism makes them move and line up. More than 150 years ago, British scientist Michael Faraday studied magnets using iron filings. He noticed that the iron filings were lined up by lines of magnetic force. Today, diagrams are drawn to show that magnetism is made up of lines of magnetic force. The north pole has a + sign (positive or plus) and the south pole a - sign (negative or minus).

You cannot see magnetic lines of force. You cannot feel them, hear, smell or taste them. People need to use magnetic objects, like paper-clips, iron filings or a compass, to see how strong a magnetic force is..

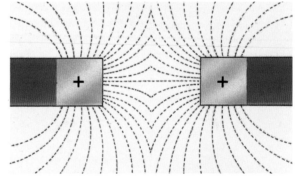

Repulsion force
Magnetic lines of force from the like poles of two magnets push against each other strongly. They can be north and north or south and south.

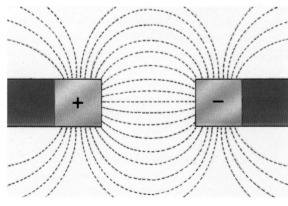

Attraction force
Magnetic lines of force from unlike poles – north and south – join and pull together powerfully. The attracting force is stronger than one magnet pulling on an ordinary iron object such as a nail.

Ring magnet
Iron filings are tiny and light. They can move about to line up with the magnetic force and they cluster where it is strongest. They show that this ring magnet has one pole on the inside of the ring and the other around the outside.

Compasses and magnetic fields

A magnetic compass usually lines up with the Earth's weak magnetism. Place a strong magnet nearby and you can overpower the Earth's magnetism and make the compass needle line up with it. However, the north end of the compass will point away from the magnet's north pole and the compass's south end from the magnet's south pole. The whole area of magnetism around any magnet, as shown by the lines of magnetic force, is called its magnetic field. Stronger magnets have bigger magnetic fields. The power of the magnetic field fades as it gets farther from its magnet.

Compass points follow lines of magnetic force from a nearby bar magnet.

Bar magnet

Iron filings line up to show how the magnetic force spreads out from the poles, or ends of the bar. The tiny particles of filings are magnetic, but not magnetized, as they do not keep their magnetism when the bar magnet is removed.

Horseshoe magnet

Iron filings reveal that the lines and strength of the magnetic force are concentrated around and between the poles at the ends of the horseshoe. There is little magnetism on the curved main body of the magnet because it is farther away from the poles.

PUSH AND PULL

You will need: scissors, adhesive tape, round plastic container, 2 magnets, elastic bands, steel washers, ruler, elastic bands.

Is a big magnet more powerful than a small one? This is not necessarily the case, because you cannot tell how powerful a magnet is just by looking at it. A magnet that is smaller than a box of matches can be stronger than one larger than a housebrick. It depends on exactly what the magnet is made of, and how it is first given its magnetism or magnetized. Every year, vast amounts of money are spent on research into new combinations of metals to make magnets that are smaller, lighter and stronger than their predecessors. These combinations are called alloys, and steel, made from iron and carbon, is a common example. This simple magnet strength-tester compares the power of different magnets.

Strength of a magnet

1 Cut off a length of adhesive tape and use it to fix the round container firmly to the work surface. This will act as the pivot, or the balancer.

2 Attach a magnet to one end of the ruler with an elastic band and some washers to the other end. Position the middle of the ruler on the balancer.

3 Hold another magnet above the first. Lower it until the ruler tilts. Measure its height above the table. The higher it is when the ruler tilts over, the stronger the magnet.

Power of a magnet

You will need: thread, drawing pins, pencil, cardboard, compasses, scissors, adhesive tape, ruler with 2 holes in it, elastic bands, sticky dots, pen, magnets.

1 Using thread attached to a pin and a pencil, or compasses, draw two large quarter-circles on the card. The distance from the pin to the edge should be the length of the ruler.

2 Draw a triangle in one quarter-circle and cut it out. Make a triangle from the second quarter-circle. Tape the two triangles together, as above.

3 Push a drawing pin through the hole at the ruler's end so it pivots. Attach elastic bands from the hole in the middle of the ruler to the quarter-circle's side, as shown. Use sticky dots to label the ends of the ruler and the poles of the magnets.

4 Stand the magnet-measurer upright. Fix one magnet to the ruler's top end with an elastic band. Bring the unlike pole of another magnet near it. How far can it pull the ruler? Stronger magnets pull it farther.

MAGNETS AND THEIR USES

MAGNETS are more complicated than they might seem at first. There are different shapes and sizes with different strengths of magnetic field. They have north and south poles that attract or repel. These features make magnets very useful. They are found in hundreds of tools, toys, machines and gadgets, from small magnets on kitchen cabinet door catches to giant magnets in huge electric motors. The magnets used in these gadgets are permanent magnets. Their magnetism lasts for years and can be used in many different ways. How many things containing magnets do you notice around your home?

Each of the bright plastic letters and numbers has a small magnet inside it. This sticks to the white board because the board is a thin sheet of metallic material containing iron.

Magnetic disk
Out of its protective case, an old-fashioned floppy disk looks like a dark plastic circle. It has a thin iron-based coating that can hold millions of bits of information as microscopic patches of magnetism.

Magnetic motor
Almost anything with an electric motor has a magnet, because magnetism is how the motor turns around. This includes electric drills, screwdrivers and similar tools, whether they use batteries for electricity, or the mains electricity supply from a wall socket.

Magnetic can-opener

Some can-openers have a magnet in an arm that touches the top of the can. As it is opened, the lid stays attached to the magnet, so you are less likely to cut yourself on its sharp edge. These food containers are made of steel coated with tin.

Magnetic holder

A magnet can attract and hold small iron or steel objects such as paper-clips, drawing pins, sewing needles and dressmaking pins. This container is designed to hold paper-clips or pins, and has a magnetic lid to attract them. If you accidentally drop some all over the floor, sweeping this magnetic lid over them helps pick them up again.

FACT BOX

• Magnets are often used in recycling. They are used to separate out cans that contain iron or iron alloys from those that are made of aluminium.

• Refrigerator doors have a magnetic strip around their edge. This sticks to the refrigerator when the door is closed, keeping it firmly in place and stopping warm air from getting inside and spoiling the food.

• Magnets prevent motor engines from becoming damaged. As oil passes through the mechanism, it picks up tiny bits of steel that are being worn away. Special magnetic plugs pick up these filings and wash them into the sump, a container for the oil.

Magnetic screwdriver

Some screwdrivers are magnetic, too. The steel shaft is a long bar magnet. This helps small steel screws to stick to the end as you use them. You can also use the screwdriver to lift small iron-containing objects out of awkward places.

MAGNETIC FISHING

MAGNETS on lines or ropes can be used to retrieve iron-containing things from awkward places. Salvage crews, for example, use huge magnets to recover pieces of wrecked ships and other equipment from the sea bed. The magnets are used where the locations are dangerous, or in murky water, mud and dark holes, where the items cannot be seen or reached without difficulty. The magnetic fishing game belows demonstrates how magnets are used in such a way.

You will need: green and purple plastic bags, felt-tip marker pen, scissors, steel paper-clips, magnets, string, wooden rods or dowels, adhesive tape, deep plate or shallow bowl, watering can, water.

This is a powerful example of how much strength a magnet can have. This magnet was displayed at a technological exhibition in London in the 1920s.

Fishing to win

1 Draw some fish shapes on to the plastic bags with the marker pen. Cut out the shapes carefully with the scissors.

2 Decorate the fish with the felt-tip marker pen. Draw scales on one side and write different numbers on the other side of each fish.

3 Attach a steel paper-clip to each fish. Make sure it is firmly attached. This will allow you to catch the fish with a magnetic rod.

4 Tie a magnet to one end of a piece of string. If you tie the string around the middle of the magnet, it will be quite secure.

5 Tape the string attached to the magnet to the end of a wooden rod with adhesive tape. Make sure it is stuck on securely.

6 Put in your fish scale-side up, and fill the plastic bowl or plate with water. You are now ready to play the fishing game.

WARNING
Keep plastic bags away from very young children, as these bags can be very dangerous.

Playing the fishing game
Each player should dangle their fishing rod over the plastic bowl. When one of the players says 'Go', lower your fishing rods into the water to catch the fish. The steel paper-clips on the fish will be attracted to the magnets on the end of the rods. Carefully lift your fish out of the pond. Each player can make their own pile of fish. When there are no fish left in the bowl, each player counts up the points on the back of their catch, and the highest score wins.

THE BIGGEST MAGNET

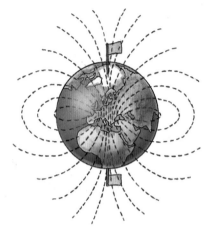

WHAT is the biggest magnet in the world? You are sitting or standing on it right now! It is the world. Planet Earth is like a giant magnet. Its magnetism is weak, however. We do not usually notice it except when magnetic compasses are used to detect it and find north and south. Then the Earth's magnetism is very useful. The force that pulls things down toward the core of the Earth and makes them fall to the ground is not magnetism. It is called gravity. It affects everything, whether it is magnetic or not.

Think of the Earth as a giant magnet spinning through Space. Its lines of magnetic force extend out into Space.

The iron core
How does the Earth make its magnetism? Scientists believe it may be due to electric currents flowing in the core, the huge and solid heart of the planet. The core is mostly made of iron and nickel, which is under enormous pressure and at a very high temperature. The flowing movements may make the magnetism, like a huge bar magnet inside the Earth.

Earth's magnetic field (lines of force)

Earth's surface

Electric currents flow slowly in the Earth's core

Earth's mantle (partly melted rocks)

Warm winds and sunshine

Winds that blow up from the south to Europe bring warm, dry air from the Sahara Desert region of North Africa. Sometimes we describe a wind by the direction that it is blowing from. The name of this direction comes from the names of the Earth's magnetic poles. Easterly and westerly winds come from directions at right angles to the North and South Poles.

Magnetic storms

Some types of storm and thundercloud have immense amounts of magnetism and electricity in them, much stronger than Earth's normal magnetic field. They are called magnetic storms. They can affect radio and television sets by disturbing the radio waves that these pick up.

Cold winds and snow

'The north wind doth blow, and we shall have snow,' goes the poem. Winds blowing from a certain direction usually bring different kinds of weather. In Europe and North America, winds from the north bring cold air, frost and snow down from the North Pole and Arctic region.

HOW A COMPASS WORKS

You will need: paper-clip, strong magnet, adhesive tape, scissors, piece of cork tile, deep plate or shallow bowl, water, ready-made compass.

I F you were a sailor or an explorer, setting off on an exciting journey into unknown lands, one of the most important things you could carry would be a compass. The compass needle is a simple magnet. It is long and thin so that it can spin freely around on a pivot. This simple instrument has saved countless lives, from people lost in the jungle or desert to sailors cast adrift at sea. It has many useful features, even compared with modern devices such as electronic satellite navigation, equipment that uses the GPS (Global Positioning System). The magnetic compass is small, simple to use and reliable. It needs no batteries or fuel. Used correctly, it is very accurate. When looked after properly, a good compass should last a lifetime.

Making a simple compass

1 Straighten out a paper-clip. Stroke it about 50 times with one pole of a magnet. Always stroke in the same direction. Tape the paper-clip, which is now a magnet, to the cork. Float it in a bowl of water.

2 The paper-clip magnet should point north and south. Its north pole is attracted to the Earth's North Pole. Check it and compare it with a ready-made compass. Is your paper-clip magnet accurate?

3 If you bring a strong magnet near to a compass, its magnetic field overpowers the Earth's magnetic field. It attracts the compass, which now lines up with the nearby magnet.

Using a compass

To use a ready-made compass, hold it level and steady so that the needle can spin freely. Let it settle and note where it points. Do this several times to check that the needle does not stick on the base or on its pivot. Carefully turn the base so the N, or north, lines up with the needle. This usually has a spot of paint or an N to indicate its north-seeking end. Compare your home-made paper-clip compass with the ready-made one. Remember that a compass needle or pointer is a magnet. What happens if you put your home-made paper-clip compass very near the ready-made compass needle? Do they swing around to point at each other? They may do, since their unlike poles will attract each other while the like ones repel.

Making a loop compass

1 Straighten out a paper-clip. Magnetize it by stroking it with the strong magnet. Cut out a circle of cardboard, bend the wire into a large loop and insert it into the card.

2 Tape the paper-clip to the piece of cork tile and then to the circle. Tie the thread to the top of the wire loop. Let it hang and twirl around freely. It is now ready to test.

3 Does the paper-clip magnet work as a compass needle and point north and south? Check it with the ready-made compass and what do you find?

THE MAGNETIC POLES

Magnetic North Pole

Geographic North Pole

Geographic South Pole

Magnetic South Pole

The Geographic Poles indicate the Earth's axis, the imaginary line around which it spins in Space. The Magnetic Poles show where the Earth's magnetism is concentrated.

THE Earth is like a giant magnet – so it must have two poles. We call them the Magnetic North Pole and the Magnetic South Pole. However, there is also another pair of poles – the Geographic North Pole and the Geographic South Pole. They are in different places from their matching Magnetic Poles. The Magnetic Poles are where a compass points to. The Geographic Poles mark the line or axis that the Earth spins around. The areas around the poles are called the polar regions. They are at the top and bottom of the world, where the Sun's warmth is very weak, so they are very cold!

A polar gap
Due to the way the Earth's magnetic field is generated, the direction of the Earth's magnetism is at a slight angle to the Earth's axis. The Magnetic North Pole lies to the west of Ellesmere Island in Canada, a few hundred kilometres/ miles from the Geographic North Pole. A compass needle points to the Magnetic North Pole.

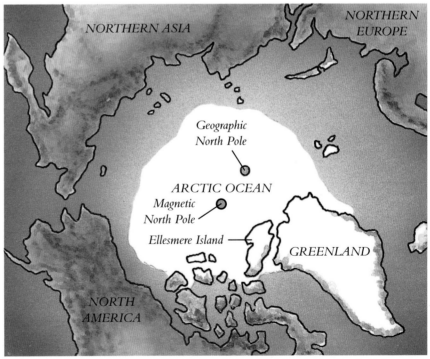

NORTHERN ASIA

NORTHERN EUROPE

Geographic North Pole

ARCTIC OCEAN

Magnetic North Pole

Ellesmere Island

GREENLAND

NORTH AMERICA

28

Race to the North Pole

The Geographic North Pole is in the middle of the Arctic Ocean, which is always covered by a layer of ice. In 1909, the American explorer Robert Peary (left) claimed to have walked there across the dangerous, shifting ice-cap. However, many experts now doubt that he reached the exact Geographic North Pole.

FACT BOX

• The Magnetic North and South Poles do not stay still. Over hundreds and thousands of years, they drift.

• Sometimes the Magnetic North and South flip, or swap over, so the Magnetic North Pole is suddenly near the Geographic South Pole, and Magnetic South Pole is near the Geographic North Pole! This is called a magnetic reversal. It has happened hundreds of times over millions of years.

• As certain kinds of rocks are formed on the Earth, they have the magnetism trapped inside them, like billions of tiny compass needles. Rocks of different ages show how the magnetic poles have moved and flipped.

Race to the South Pole

The Geographic South Pole is on the great southern continent of Antarctica, which is completely covered by thick ice for nearly all of the year. In 1911, two teams of explorers raced to get there. Norwegian Roald Amundsen's group was first, and returned safely. British Robert Falcon Scott's (right) expedition arrived one month later. On arrival, they found a sympathetic note from Amundsen. Sadly, Scott and his men did not survive the return journey.

Fossil ferns in the snow
The land near the North Pole is now snow-covered. Millions of years ago it was warm so that ferns and plants flourished.

MAGNETS IN SPACE

Van Allen belts

The magnetosphere is the region in Space around the Earth where the solar wind from the Sun blows through the Earth's magnetic field. It is like a giant lop-sided doughnut. It has several layers, including the Van Allen belts, named after the scientist who discovered them using satellite information.

THE Earth's magnetism is not just down on the ground, where we detect it with compasses. Like any other magnet, the Earth's magnetic field extends away from it, into the air – and even right out into Space. But the magnetic field is not equal on both sides of the planet, as it is with most ordinary magnets. A stream of energy and particles from the Sun, called the solar wind, blows against the magnetic field and makes it lop-sided. This vast region, where the magnetic field meets the solar wind, is called the magnetosphere. It extends for thousands of kilometres into Space, especially on the night side of the Earth, away from the Sun.

Magnetism in deep Space

Powerful telescopes and satellite equipment show that there is magnetism deep in Space. It is usually concentrated around incredibly vast objects like galaxies and quasars. The magnetism is powerful, billions of times stronger than any magnets made on Earth.

Finding the field

In 1958, one of the first satellites, *Explorer 1*, detected magnetic layers around the Earth. In the early 1960s, *Explorer 12* proved that the magnetosphere existed. Its scientific instruments detected the magnetism and energy far into Space, and how these varied.

Lights in the sky
Strange, shimmering lights sometimes appear in the sky near the North and South Poles. They are called the Northern Lights, or Aurora Borealis, and the Southern Lights, or Aurora Australis. They are due to magnetism, electricity and particles very high above, almost in Space.

The planets
Several planets in our Solar System are magnetic. They have their own magnetic fields and magnetospheres like Earth. They include the small planet nearest the Sun, called Mercury, and the giant planets much farther away, Jupiter and Saturn *(above)*.

Space walk
Magnetism in Space is sometimes very useful. Astronauts use magnetic holders to stop things drifting around in the weightless conditions inside the spacecraft. Outside, during a Space walk, magnetic boots, gloves and holders stop things drifting away into Space. That includes the astronaut!

MAGNETS AND MAPS

OOK at a map – which way up does it go? Maps are made according to the Earth's magnetism and the magnetic compass. They have north at the top, in the same way that the North Pole is at the top of the world. We are used to looking at maps and using them with north at the top, pointing straight up or away from us. Look on a local map to find a diagram of the compass points, an arrow or N that indicates north. Then, using a compass, turn the map so that its north faces the same way as the compass north. Now the map is lined up accurately in relation to the landscape. If you are on a hilltop with wide views, you can see how the map is a tiny version of the countryside all around.

Maps are important because they enable us to know where we are going. Without magnets we would not know how to use a map or find our way around.

Which way up?

We are so familiar with maps having north at the top, that they look odd when they are turned around. Can you recognize this country *(left)* when it is turned upside down? Can you find it on the globe *(right)*?

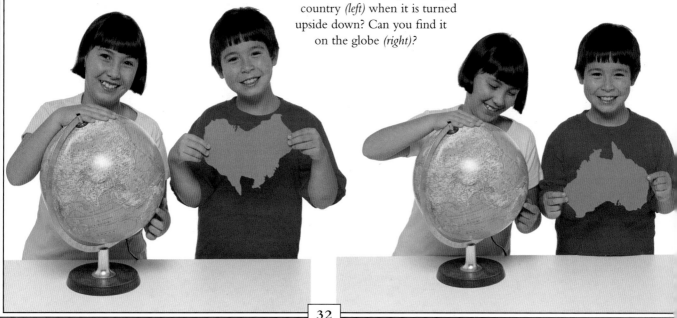

The compass maze

Can you find your way through this maze? When you have made it to the other side, try recording your route with compass points. At the beginning of the journey, you head east, turn north and then go east again. Can you complete these instructions for the entire journey?

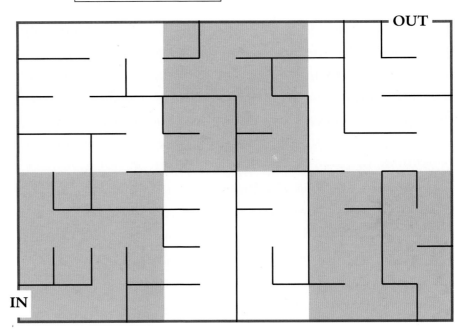

OUT

IN

Drawing a maze

MATERIALS

You will need: cardboard, felt-tipped pens, compass.

1 Draw your own maze. Make it bright and fun. Put in some dead ends and false turns. Make sure that one route leads all the way through from one end of the maze to the other, even though the way may be very twisty!

2 Now record your course through the maze, using compass points for the directions. You can limit the information to north, south, east and west, or include more detailed directions such as north-east and south-west.

MAGNETIC SENSE

Magnetism is probably an important guide to the Arctic tern on its migratory route. It flies to the far north of the Arctic for the summer. To avoid the long northern winter, it flies around the world to the far south, even to Antarctica.

WE cannot detect magnets or magnetic fields with our own bodies. However, various animals seem to sense magnetism. They may detect the Earth's magnetic field and use it to help them navigate, or find their way, on very long journeys called migrations. Like human sailors or explorers using a magnetic compass, migrating animals seem to have a built-in body compass. Many kinds of animals migrate. They include swallows, geese and various other birds, fish, like salmon, and large mammals such as whales, seals and caribou. Scientists have found tiny iron particles in the heads of some animals, such as fish, that may act as a natural compass.

Migration route
The tern's migration follows the Earth's lines of magnetic force. It flies from north to south and then returns later in the year, from south to north. Birds probably use several clues to navigate, such as rivers, mountains, coastlines, the positions of the Sun, Moon and stars, as well as magnetism.

Whales at sea
Many great whales and other types of sea mammal go on long, annual journeys. They usually start from their winter habitat of warm tropical sea and move to their summer habitat of polar seas, where food is plentiful. Like other migrating sea animals, they probably use several clues to find their way, such as coastlines, undersea mountains or cliffs, sea currents, the Earth's gravity and magnetism.

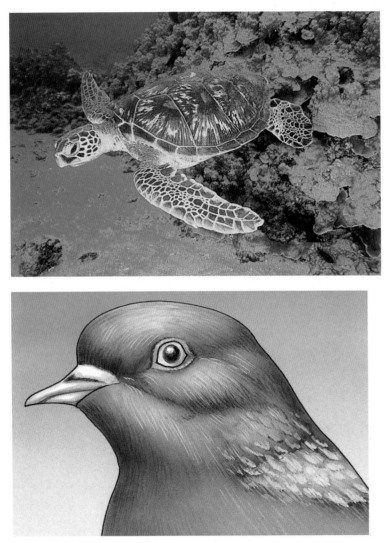

Turtle recall
Sea turtles also wander the world's oceans, yet they return to the beach where they hatched from eggs, to lay their own eggs.

To the north
The usual reason for migration is to travel to a place where conditions are good for a limited time. In the short Arctic summer, plants grow quickly and plentifully. Birds such as geese fly there to breed. Insects such as the monarch butterfly also go on long annual migrations.

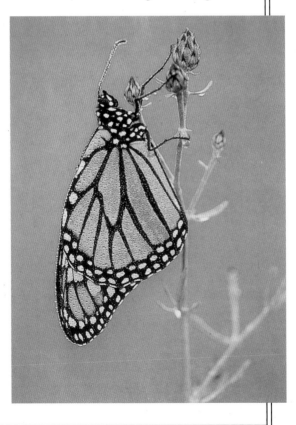

Where is the body compass?
Tiny pieces or particles of iron have been found in various parts of the body in pigeons, including the eyes, brain and upper beak. Testing whether any of these areas works as a built-in compass is very difficult. However, when scientists strapped a small but strong magnet to a pigeon's head, it interfered with the bird's ability to navigate.

ELECTRIC MAGNETS

The magnetic field around a wire with electricity flowing through it can be made stronger by wrapping the wire in a coil around an iron bar. The iron bar then works like a bar magnet – but only while electricity flows. This simple device, the electromagnet, is a magnet that you can switch on and off. Electromagnets are found in their millions in all kinds of machinery.

THE ordinary bar and horseshoe magnets are permanent magnets. They have what scientists call spontaneous permanent magnetism. Their magnetism needs no outside force or energy. But there is another way of making magnetism – by electricity. When electricity flows through a wire or another similar conductor (electricity-carrier), it produces a magnetic field around the wire. This is called electromagnetism or EM. In fact, magnetism and electricity are very closely linked. Each can be used to make the other. EM is used in thousands of different tools, machines and devices that are vital in our modern world.

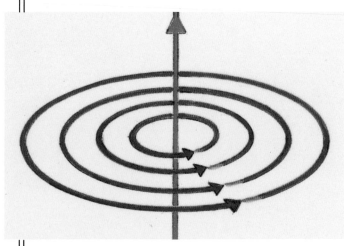

Creating a magnetic field
As electricity flows through a wire, a magnetic field is created around it. The magnetic lines of force flow in circles around the wire. This is called an electromagnetic field. As soon as the electricity is switched off, the magnetism stops.

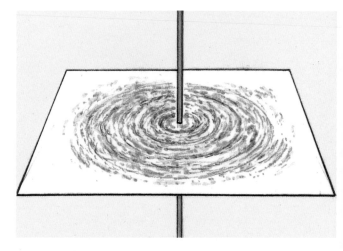

Seeing electromagnetism
If iron filings are sprinkled on to a piece of cardboard that has an electricity-carrying wire through it, the filings are affected by the magnetic field. They arrange themselves in circles to show the lines of magnetic force, as they do with an ordinary magnet.

EM in toys

Many toys have electromagnets inside them. This battery-operated car is steered by using two electromagnets at the front. One twists the wheels so the car turns left and the other makes it go to the right. With both of the electromagnets switched off, a spring pulls the wheels so the car goes straight.

FACT BOX

• In Denmark, the scientist Hans Christian Oersted (1777-1851) was the first to discover that an electric current produced magnetism, in 1820. During a talk to students, he noticed that a compass needle was affected by a nearby electricity-carrying wire.

• In France, André Marie Ampère (1775-1836) did many experiments on electricity and magnetism. He invented the idea of twisting wire into a coil, called a solenoid, to make its magnetism stronger.

• In England, Michael Faraday (1791-1867) discovered electromagnetic induction, using magnetism to generate an electic current. This led to many useful inventions, including the electric motor, dynamo and transformer.

• In the USA, Joseph Henry (1797-1878) also discovered electromagnetic induction and how to make an electric motor. He made incredibly powerful electromagnets that lifted weights of over one tonne.

Switch on and off

One of the most useful features of an electromagnet is that you can switch it on and off. Large electromagnets are strong enough to pick up old cars by their steel roofs and drop them into the car-crusher. Many machines and equipment rely on electromagnets for their effectiveness.

MAKING AN ELECTROMAGNET

THE magnetism of an electromagnet is the same as magnetism from an ordinary magnet. It is just the way of making it that differs. The first practical, useful electromagnets were made by British bootmaker and spare-time scientist William Sturgeon in the 1820s to amaze audiences at his science shows. The basic design has hardly changed since. You can make a similar electromagnet and amaze your friends, too!

You will need: wire-strippers, about two metres (two yards) of ordinary wire (insulated, plastic-coated, multi-strand copper), large iron nail, bar or rod, 9-volt battery, paper-clips, piece of cardboad, brass split-pin fasteners.

1925-816

William Sturgeon's original electromagnet was not very different from this version!

Your own electromagnet

1 Using the wire-strippers, carefully remove 5 centimetres (2 inches) of plastic insulation from each end of the wire. These bare ends will connect to the battery.

2 Carefully wrap the wire in a tight coil around the iron nail. The insulation around the wire stops the electricity leaking into the iron nail.

3 Connect the wire's ends to the battery terminals. (It does not matter which is positive or negative.) Test your electromagnet by picking up paper-clips.

Stronger magnets

This electromagnet *(left)* has two sets of coils, one on top of the other, but all made from one length of wire. There are several ways of making an electromagnet stronger and more powerful. One is to put more turns of wire on to the central iron rod or bar. You could try making your own version of this with a longer piece of wire. Wrap one set of turns around the nail. Then make another set of turns to form a second coil on top of the first. Another way is to use more electricity, such as two 9-volt batteries. In this project electricity flows as soon as the wires are joined to the battery. This can quickly make the battery run down or flat. It is better to have a switch, so you can turn the electromagnet on and off easily, as needed.

WARNING

NEVER try using electricity from the mains socket on the wall. It is far too dangerous and could kill. Ask an adult for help in this project.

Adding a switch

1 Make two equal-sized holes in the piece of cardboard. Push the brass split-pins into them. Push one of the split-pins through a paper-clip first. Open out the legs of the split-pins. Each leg is now ready to connect to your electromagnet.

2 Connect one end of the electromagnet wire to the split-pin. Connect the other to a battery terminal. Join the remaining split-pin to the other battery terminal with another short piece of wire. Turn the cardboard over.

3 The paper-clip fixed to one split-pin is the switch. Push it away from the other split-pin and notice that no electricity flows to the nail. Turn the paper-clip to touch the split-pin. Electricity flows, switching on the electromagnet.

EM MACHINES

Hundreds of machines use the switchable on-off magnetic power of electromagnetism. You can find them around the home, at school, in factories and offices, in the car, the garage, the supermarket – just about everywhere. Some electromagnetic machines use the electricity from batteries. Others need the much more powerful mains electricity from wall sockets.

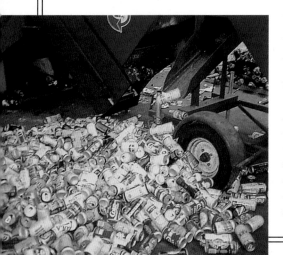

A metal detector uses electromagnetism to signal if iron-containing substances are nearby. Some detectors can also locate other types of metals. They work by battery power.

Medical scanners

The magnetic resonance imager (MRI) is a type of scanner that can see inside the body. The person is put into a huge electromagnet, which uses a combination of magnetism and radio waves to detect different parts inside the body. A computer processes the results and shows them on a screen.

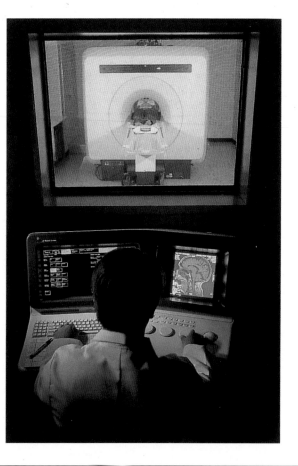

Recycling

At some recycling points, aluminium drinks cans and steel food cans all go into the same container. At the recycling depot, an electromagnet separates them by attracting the steel cans but not the aluminium ones.

Smashing atoms

The world's biggest set of electromagnets are part of the world's biggest machine – the Large Hadron Collider (LHC). This is a tube similar to the short section on the left, but curved to make a circle 27 kilometres (16.8 miles) long. The LHC is buried deep underground near Geneva, Switzerland. Since 2009 scientists have been using it to smash together bits of atoms – particles that make up everything in the Universe.

Inside the LHC

The LHC has more than 1,600 electromagnets in its long tube. They can be made stronger or weaker, or switched on and off at amazing speed. These electromagnets affect the tiniest bits of atomic particles, such as protons, making them whizz through the tube at incredible speed. The protons collide with (smash into) each other or with other particles. The collisions produce various types of energy, beams and more particles. The results are helping scientists to study what is inside the different pieces of atoms and other matter.

Cooling pipe

Iron parts of electromagnets

Coils of electromagnets

Twin beams of particles (protons)

Protons travel in opposite directions

3.8 metre- (12.5 foot-) wide outer tunnel

LHC tube

Heatproof lining

"Beam pipes" for high-energy particles

THE EM OLYMPICS

ELECTROMAGNETS are found in many toys and games. You can use the power of electromagnetism to make your own game, the EM Olympics. Here, the washer represents a discus, the nut a shot-put and the nail a javelin. The electromagnet is used to throw each of them. The secret of success is in the timing. At the exact moment when you switch off the electromagnet, it stops attracting the iron or steel object and releases it.

Throwing a real javelin is one of several Olympic field events. The sport probably began in ancient times with spears.

M A T E R I A L S

You will need: cereal box (if using), sheets of cardboard, scissors, glue, marker pen, decorative stick-on shapes, large iron nail, insulated (plastic-coated) copper wire, wire-strippers, paper-clip, brass split-pin fasteners, battery, adhesive tape, washer, small nails, nut.

The EM Games

1 Cut the front panel from a large cereal box, and paint the sides and back if you wish. Glue the top flap down. Alternatively, make a box of the same dimensions from cardboard.

2 Cut out squares of cardboard for the scoreboard and tape them together to make a sheet that will fit neatly into the box. Write scores on them and decorate them.

3 Fit the scoreboard into the box. It is best not to glue it, since you may wish to take it out and alter the scores, or make a new scoreboard as you become an expert at the games.

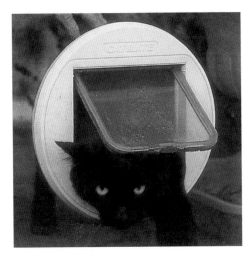

A cat's entrance door
This type of cat flap can be opened only by a cat wearing a special collar with an electromagnet attached to it. A switch is flicked when the cat pushes against the flap.

4 Cut out two more long, wide strips of cardboard. Tape them together at two of their short edges. Glue the other short edges inside the box, on opposite sides. Position this 'arch' at one end of the box.

5 Make an electromagnet (as shown on page 38). Tape it to the arch so it can hang below by its wires. Connect the free ends of the wire to the battery. Use a paper-clip to make a switch for the battery.

6 Push the nail electromagnet to and fro to test that it swings freely. In turn, put iron or steel objects in the box – use a nail as a javelin, a nut as a shot-put and a washer as a discus. Switch on the nail electromagnet. Push the nail electromagnet to make it swing. As it moves, it should pull the items in the box with it. Turn off the switch and they will be released. Note where they land on the scoreboard.

MAGNETISM IN MOTORS

T HE electric motor changes electricity, using magnetism, into a turning or spinning force that has thousands of uses. There is also a machine that does the opposite. It changes a turning force, using magnetism, into electricity. This is called a dynamo or generator. It is this machine that makes electricity in power stations. Electromagnetic machines such as the motor and generator are essential to modern life.

This simple piece of equipment is a metal ring wrapped in coils of wire. Michael Faraday and other scientists used it to study electricity and magnetism. With its help they invented machines such as the electric motor, dynamo, generator and transformer.

Electric motor

An electric motor has a wire coil positioned between permanent magnets. Electricity flows and makes the coil an electromagnet. The electricity's direction means that the coil's magnetic poles are the same as the nearest poles of the permanent magnet - and, as we know, like poles repel. So the coil spins around. However, the two-part turning contact called the commutator spins with the coil and reverses the electricity's direction. This reverses the coil's electro-magnetic poles, while the permanent magnet's poles stay the same. Again, like poles repel, so the coil twirls a bit more. The commutator reverses the electricity again and a cycle is set up.

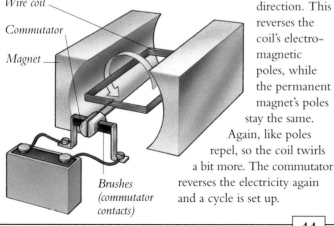

Wire coil
Commutator
Magnet
Brushes (commutator contacts)

Turning force
Wire coil
Commutator
Magnet
Brushes (commutator contacts)

Electric dynamo or generator

A dynamo has almost exactly the same parts as an electric motor. But the coil is turned around by an outside force, such as a petrol engine, a steam turbine, or even a handle turned by hand! As the coil turns around in the magnetic field of the permanent magnet, electricity is generated in its wires. This is called electromagnetic induction.

Big motors

Electric trains, like this subway train, have huge electric motors to turn the wheels around. Each pair of wheels on their axle has their own motor.

Green energy

Wind turbines use electromagnetic induction to harness natural wind power. The wind's energy turns the rotor blades, which are connected to an electrical generator in the "pod" just behind them. The generator has two sets of wire coils, one inside the other, like spinning electromagnets. As the rotors turn one set of coils, electricity is produced in the other set.

Big generators

The giant generators in power stations turn the energy of movement into the energy of electricity. The turning movement usually comes from burning fuel (coal, gas, or oil) to heat water into steam. This rushes past the fan-like blades of a huge turbine and makes it spin.

MOTORIZED MACHINES

How many electric motors are near you, right now? There are probably more than you realize. In a house packed with gadgets, there are motors in the washing machine, tumble-dryer, dishwasher, microwave oven turntable, vacuum cleaner, electric food mixer, electric can-opener, central heating pump, cooling fan, CD player, computer or laptop disk drive, DVD player, toys such as cars and robots - the list is very long! Next time you are in a classroom, workshop, garage, office, factory or similar place, see how many electric motors you can spot.

Brushing

An electric toothbrush has a small motor inside it, in the handle near the batteries. It turns an arm mechanism that makes the brush head vibrate or move side to side very rapidly.

Blowing

An electric motor in a hair-dryer turns a fan that blows cool air through the fan's heater to make it warm. Warm air blows out of the nozzle. A switch alters the amount of electricity fed to the fan motor to change the amount of blown air.

Super charger

Most toy cars and trucks work by electric motors. The motor spins around and turns the wheels, usually through a set of gears to slow down the spinning speed. Many larger vehicles, including some cars, taxis, buses and delivery vans, are now partially or entirely powered by electric motors.

FACT BOX

- There are two main kinds of electric motor. The DC, or direct current, motor works using electricity that flows steadily in one direction, like the electricity from a battery.

- The AC, or alternating current, motor works using electricity that changes or reverses its direction of flow 50 times each second. Mains electricity from a wall socket does this.

- The smallest electric motors are tinier than a pinhead. They are part of the new technology of nano-machinery. They are used to test new methods in science, engineering and medicine.

- Some of the biggest electric motors are used on electric trains and in heavy engineering such as blast furnaces for making iron and steel.

- Each time you use a lift, you are pulled up or lowered down by an electric motor.

Drilling

The electric drill has a strong motor that twists the drill bit around so it can bore holes in wood, brick and even concrete. Similar motors are used in many other electric tools and appliances, such as electric saws, screwdrivers, sanders, mowers, strimmers and hedge-trimmers.

Getting started

Without the large and powerful electric motor that turns the engine to start a car, you would have to start it by turning a handle! A modern car has dozens of other electric motors to work the fuel pump, windscreen wipers, CD player, electric windows, electric seat adjusters and many other things. The list is almost endless.

SOUND TO MAGNETISM

Coil of electromagnet

Parchment sheet

We have seen that movement can be converted into electricity, using magnetism. When a wire or similar object moves within the magnetic field of a magnet, the wire passes or cuts the lines of magnetic force. As it does so, electricity is generated in the wire. The process is called electromagnetic induction. It is used in many machines and devices, such as dynamos or generators and electric guitars. Sound is a type of movement. It is the to-and-fro vibrations in air. Sound can be converted into electricity too, using magnetism. In the 1870s, Alexander Graham Bell invented the first telephone using a combination of sound, magnetism and electricity.

In the first telephones, sound waves from the voice hit a large piece of parchment paper that was stretched tight like a drum skin. This made it vibrate. The paper was attached to a magnet, which also vibrated – within a wire coil. The magnet moving near the coil created electricity in the coil.

Diaphragm (flat sheet)

Coil

Magnet

On the line
Phones of all kinds have a mouthpiece that picks up the sounds of your voice and changes them to electricity. It works in a different way to the mouthpiece of the early telephone. However, the earpiece still works as a type of small loudspeaker.

Microphone
A microphone is a device that detects patterns of sound waves and turns them into corresponding patterns of electricity. Some microphones, such as the moving-coil version shown here, use magnetism. Others, like the carbon button microphone in the mouthpiece of a telephone, work in a different way.

Early microphones
The early microphones used by radio stations were very large and cumbersome. The one shown on the left dates back to 1924.

Hand-held microphones
Microphones have become easier and smaller to move around. They also pick up sounds more accurately.

Two-way radio
Walkie-talkies *(right)*, two-way radios and mobile phones all use microphones and loudspeakers. These types of microphones are designed to be simple, tough and reliable. They pick up the sounds of the human voice. Other microphones are designed to pick up the sounds of musical instruments such as a piano or violin.

Coils of wire

Stylus (needle)

Two tiny bar-shaped magnets

Vinyl pick-up
Vinyl records were the primary medium used for music reproduction for most of the 20th century and continue to be made and sold today. They are usually played using a moving-coil magnetic pick-up. This has a tiny pointed stylus needle that vibrates as it follows the wavy groove on the record. The vibrations shake two tiny bar-shaped magnets inside. Their magnetic fields affect small coils of wire nearby, creating patterns of electricity that follow the patterns of vibrations.

MAGNETS AS STORAGE SPACE

Patches of magnetism on tape are codes for sounds

Magnetic tape stores sounds as micro-dots of magnetism. In fact, the tape stores any kind of information or data in this way, in the form of codes, including sounds, computer programs and files, text and pictures.

RECORDED music and sound are part of our daily life. We tune into music, speech and other sounds on the radio and television that have been recorded earlier on tape. Without magnetism, these tapes would not be possible. The sounds are recorded, or stored, as tiny patches of magnetism, which are far too small to see. These patches stay in the tape for many years without fading. The process of recording sounds and then pictures on magnetic tape began in the 1930s. Tape is still used in the media industry today, in formats such as Sony's D-5 HD and HDCAM. A magnetic tape has several layers. The base is strong, flexible plastic. The magnetic layer has tiny particles of iron-containing substances such as iron oxide, often mixed with other metals such as chrome, to improve the quality.

Tape head spins around one way

Guide pins

Tape passes head other way

Magnetic tape

Tape head
In some types of tape recorders, the record and playback heads were the same device. The head spun around one way as the magnetic tape moved past it the other way. Video tape and digital audio tape (DAT) also used these types of rotating heads.

FACT BOX
• The first magnetic sound-recorder was invented in 1898, by Valdemar Poulsen. It was not a tape recorder, but a wire recorder, using a long piece of steel wire.

• The first tape recorders used metal tape. They were invented in 1928.

• In the 1930s, the tape was changed from metal to plastic with a very thin iron coating. This is the type of tape used today.

• Sounds can also be recorded or stored non-magnetically – as a wavy groove in a vinyl record disc, or as tiny lumps and pits read by laser light, on a CD.

Flash drive
'Memory sticks' or 'pen drives', also called flash memory, use the tiniest parts of atoms – electrons. Each electron is like an incredibly small magnet with just one charge, negative (like a magnet's south pole). Positive charges nearby make the electrons move into positions that represent information.

Recording studio
The sound engineer sits in the control room at a huge desk called the mixing console, with the performers in a separate sound-proofed studio room. Some studios use DAT, digital audio tape, to store the sounds magnetically. The sounds from each different instrument are then combined or mixed for the best result.

RAM chips
Computers use RAM (Random-Access Memory) to store information that can then be changed. RAM is based on electrons, as described for flash drives, above right. These negative bits of atoms are moved around by electronic components known as transistors and capacitors, built into microchips.

Microchip circuit board
Electronic devices like computers and mobile phones use flowing electrons, rather than moving mechanical parts such as spinning magnets and wire coils. On a circuit board RAM, ROM (Read-Only Memory) and many other kinds of microchips, each with thousands of microscopic-sized components, are connected by narrow strips of metal.

MAGNETISM AND SOUND

HOWEVER sounds are recorded, from old-style vinyl records to the latest microchip flash drives, at some stage we usually want to listen to, or play back, the sounds again. The basic devices for doing this are loudspeakers and earphones – and they also rely on magnetism. They come in many shapes and sizes, from speakers larger than a tabletop for giant stage shows and events, to mini-speakers smaller than this letter 'o', in the earpieces of earphones, and in mobile phones and other types of telephones.

Wires carrying electricity

Wire coil

Case

Magnet

Frame

Moving cone

Inside a loudspeaker

Patterns of varying electrical signals are transferred to the loudspeaker along the connecting wire or speaker lead. They go through the wire coil, which is attached to the large card or plastic speaker cone. The signals make the coil into an electromagnet that varies in strength. This magnetic field is itself inside the field of a strong permanent magnet. The two fields interact, with like poles repelling in the usual way. This makes the coil move or vibrate to and fro, which makes the loudspeaker cone vibrate too. This, in turn, sends out sound waves.

Headphones

Small, lightweight, personal headphones, in-ear phones and earbuds work in a similar way to loudspeakers. They use powerful magnets made from an alloy (mixture) of three metals – neodymium, iron and boron, called NIB. This allows the magnets in the earpieces to be far smaller and lighter. Magnets made of ordinary iron or steel would be too big and heavy.

Wire coil

Head band

Diaphragm (thin sheet)

Case

Samarium-cobalt magnet

Wires

Spongy earpiece

Telephone earpiece

The earpiece of a telephone receives varying patterns of electrical signals from the mouthpiece of the telephone held by the person at the other end of the line. The earpiece works like a simple loudspeaker to recreate the sounds of the other person's voice.

Big and small

Large loudspeakers, sometimes 40 centimetres (2 feet) across, produce low or deep sounds best, as from a bass guitar or drum. They are called woofers. Small loudspeakers only a few centimetres across are known as tweeters. They produce high or shrill sounds best, such as cymbals and flutes. Most hi-fi loudspeakers contain both a woofer and tweeter. They may also have a mid-range loudspeaker. This helps to reproduce medium-pitched sounds and notes clearly.

MAGNETIC MUSIC

WITHOUT magnetism, we would not have the sound of the electric guitar, and rock music would be very different! An acoustic guitar's sound comes from its vibrating strings, which are made louder by the guitar's hollow body. When you play an electric guitar, it actually sounds very quiet and tinny. An electric guitar uses electromagnetism to make small electrical signals. The guitar is plugged into an amplifier and the signals are fed into it. The amplifier makes these signals stronger and in turn sends them to a loudspeaker (another electromagnetic device) which makes the electrical signals into actual sounds.

If an electric guitar is not plugged in, its strings are quiet and shrill when they are plucked. The heavy, solid body of the guitar does not make the strings louder, unlike the hollow, thin-walled body of an acoustic guitar.

Tuning keys

Head

Neck

Strings

Frets

Magnetic pick-ups

Bridge and protective plate

Body

Socket for pick-up lead

Selector switch

Volume knob

Tone knobs

Parts of the guitar
A typical electric guitar has strings on its long neck and a thick, solid body. The electromagnetic pick-ups are under the strings in the body. These make electrical signals when the strings vibrate. The volume knob makes the signals quieter, stronger or weaker and the tone knobs make the sound higher and shriller, or lower and duller. The selector switch turns the various pick-ups on or off.

The pick-up

An electric guitar's pick-up has a plastic cover. Underneath are six small bar-shaped, permanent magnets called pole pieces, with a coil of wire wrapped around them. In many guitars this coil has more than 6,000 turns!

Cover

Pole pieces

Coil of wire inside pick-up

Ends of wire coil connected to wire that goes to plug socket

Base

How the pick-up works

The permanent magnets create a magnetic field around the pick-up. When the metal guitar string is plucked, it vibrates in this field and disturbs it. The variations in magnetism create electrical signals in the wire coil by the process of electromagnetic induction.

Metal vibrating strings alter magnetic field

Electric piano

Some electric pianos work in the same way as an electric guitar. When you press a key, this plucks a small strip of metal called a reed, making it ping and vibrate. The reed is next to a small magnet wrapped in a wire coil. It creates electrical signals in the same way as the guitar pick-up above. There are also magnets and electromagnets inside modern electronic synthesizers, keyboards and organs.

FACT BOX

• The first guitars with electromagnetic pick-ups were made in the 1930s. One of the earliest was the 1931 *Frying Pan*, shaped like a banjo. It had a pick-up consisting of two horseshoe magnets around a coil of wire.

• The first mass-produced electric guitars were made in 1932 by a company set up by Adolph Rickenbacker.

• The Gibson company started making their designs of electric guitars in about 1935, but these had hollow bodies.

• In 1950 the Fender company launched the *Broadcaster* – the first electric guitar with a solid body, bolt-on neck and two pick-ups. The rock guitar was born!

MAGNETS AND COMPUTERS

More on less

The amount of information that can be stored on disks increases every year. The words and pictures in many piles of books can fit on to one DVD. However, you can only read the disk using an electronic device, such as a computer, or a DVD or Blu-ray player. You can read a book with just your eyes!

SWITCH on a typical computer and immediately magnetism goes into action. The hard disk and perhaps the CD (compact disk) or DVD (digital versatile disk) spin around in their drives, which use magnetism in their electric motors. A type of electromagnet called the read-write head reads, or receives, the information from the hard disk so the computer can start working. Programs and other data are also stored on the hard disk as microscopic patterns of magnetism. A hard disk known as 1 TB (terabyte) can store 350 hours of ordinary television shows, or 100 hours of HD (high definition) TV. If the computer has a cooling fan, this too has an electric motor that works by magnetism.

Disk drive

The central hole of a DVD or CD fits over the drive of a special electric motor called a stepper motor. It can spin around very fast, up to 25 times every second, and yet it also stops on a spot 50 times smaller than the dot on this letter 'i'.

Compact disk

A compact disk has patterns of microscopic bumps. Like the magnetic patches on a magnetic disk, they contain information in coded form. The CD itself does not use magnetism – it is read by a laser beam. It spins around using electromagnetism, in an electric motor (*right*). The surface of a compact disk has millions of tiny bumps. A laser beam shines at these. It reflects from the patches between the bumps, but not from the bumps. The pattern of reflections is picked up by the detector.

Close-up of pits

Pits and bumps on lower surface of CD

Reading a CD

The CD drive uses a laser beam that shines at the CD's lower surface. It is reflected by the pattern of microscopic pits as the disk spins around driven by an electric motor. The detector picks up the on-off patterns of reflections and converts them into electrical signals for the computer.

Laser read head

Beam reflects

Path of beam

Prism

Laser beam

Direct or reflected beam

Motor

Read-write head

A magnetic disk read-write head works by swivelling sideways across the spinning disk to detect microscopic patterns of magnetism, and then turning them into electrical signals for the computer. It writes on to the disk in a similar way, by erasing old magnetic patches and putting new ones on it.

Storage space

The room needed for computer memory has reduced millions of times in recent years, while information is called up thousands of times faster. Massive amounts of information was once stored on large reels of magnetic tape or disks (*left*). These are called storage media. Nowadays, even more data can be held on much smaller media, such as servers (*right*).

MAGNETIC *FORMULA 1*

Real Grand Prix cars can travel 300 kilometres (200 miles) per hour, a little faster than a table-top version! They do not use magnetism in their motors as their engines run on petrol-based fuel.

A *FORMULA 1* Grand Prix car race is one of the most spectacular events in sport. Racing requires skill and determination. You can make your own table-top version and race your friends, using a few scraps of cardboard, other objects and some magnets. Remember your version is special because it uses magnetism. Small, flat bar or ring magnets are best. The trick is to stay on the track and speed along, but not so fast that the magnet loses your car! If that happens, you are out of the race and the game is over. Good luck!

Magnetic racing

1 Glue a magnet to the end of each ruler. Use 30-centimetre (12-inch) rulers if you can, or similar sized strips of wood.

2 Draw the shapes of racing cars on the cardboard. You can make the wheels a different shade, and perhaps add stripes, too.

3 Carefully cut out the car shapes with scissors. Decorate them with adhesive shapes to make up your own racing team.

M A T E R I A L S

You will need: small ring or bar magnets, glue, two long rulers or strips of wood, sheets of cardboard, pens, scissors, adhesive stars or similar shapes, paper-clips, large sheet of stiff cardboard.

4 Glue a steel paper-clip to the underside of each car. Let the glue dry thoroughly while you make the racing track from cardboard.

5 Draw a circuit on the cardboard to make the track. Put the whole track on two books so that it is raised all around the edge. This lets you get the ruler and magnet underneath. Place your racing cars on the start line. Push the ruler underneath so that the magnet faces upwards and attracts the paper-clip on the base of your car. Move the ruler slowly so that the magnet drags the paper-clip and car along. Get practice driving like this for a while. Overtaking is tricky, since you have to guide your ruler past your opponent's ruler. Good luck!

MAGNETS OF THE FUTURE

THE science of magnets and magnetism never stands still. Every day people are doing tests and experiments to make more powerful magnets, with better combinations of metals and improved designs of wire coils. Progress in electromagnets helps to design better medical scanners, atom-smashers and electric motors for all kinds of equipment and machinery. In the future, magnets will become even more important in our world.

More recent electromagnets (left) use special combinations of metals and incredible amounts of electricity. They are super-cooled to allow the electricity to flow around the wire coil more easily. They produce magnetic fields that last only a fraction of a second. Yet they have the same energy as an exploding bomb.

Region of strongest magnetism in centre

Wire coils

Super-cooled casing

Plasma power

A new design for a power station involves heating substances to incredibly high temperatures so that they are not solid, or liquid, or gas, but a different form of matter – plasma. The plasma is so hot and dangerous that it cannot touch the sides of the reactor. It is kept imprisoned in the space in the middle by intense magnetic fields.

Supermagnetism in wall of ring-shaped plasma container

Gap between plasma and wall caused by magnetism

Plasma inside magnetic field

Central supermagnet core

Base

Launched into Space

A huge magnet-powered super gun could launch a satellite. It would have a very long barrel with powerful ring-shaped electromagnets at intervals along its length, switched on and off, one after the other. These would attract the satellite in its bullet casing, speed it up along the barrel, stage by stage, finally hurling it with amazing force and speed into Space.

Launcher with satellite or missile inside

Supermagnet ring switches on and off rapidly

Unmagnetized portion

Supermagnet rings come on and off one by one and pull the launcher at an ever increasing speed up the gun barrel

Helping the environment

Recycling is important, to save natural resources on Earth. Magnets and electromagnets help by sorting out metals and moving them around in the scrapyard, so that they can be melted down and reused.

More for less

Better designs of electromagnets help in many ways. In the generators of power stations, they can help to make more electricity using less fuel. Improved electromagnets in all kinds of machines use less electricity, yet produce more magnetism.

TRICKS WITH MAGNETS

MANY amazing and magic-like tricks rely on the invisible power of magnets. For example, did you know you can easily remove paper-clips from water without getting your fingers wet, or that you can make a paper bat that hovers unsupported in mid-air? These ideas are guaranteed to intrigue your friends. After learning about magnets in this book, you will probably be able to come up with lots more ideas of your own. Ask your friends, too, if they have any tricks that use the powers of simple magnets to such fascinating effect.

It is not difficult to do tricks with magnets, if you have the right materials handy.

MATERIALS

You will need: paper-clips, glass of water, magnet.

Fun with magnets

1 Put the paper-clips into the glass of water. Place the magnet against the glass's side. It should attract a paper-clip because magnetism is passing through the glass.

2 Slowly slide the magnet up the side of the glass. Do this carefully and the paper-clip will follow, attracted and dragged along by the magnet.

3 Keep sliding the magnet until it reaches the rim of the glass. Now lift away the paper-clip. One by one, do the same with the rest of the paper-clips.

Bat magnet

You will need: black paper, white pencil, scissors, stiff green paper, adhesive tape, stiff wire, paper-clips, string, strong magnet.

1 Draw a large bat shape on to a sheet of black paper with the white pencil. Cut it out.

2 Tape stiff paper to the bat's underside, and stiff wire across the wings. Secure a piece of string.

3 Place several paper-clips on the paper used to stiffen the bat. Cover each clip with a piece of adhesive tape to keep it secure.

4 Lift the bat from the top side with the magnet by attracting the paper-clips through the paper. As the bat rises, the string lengthens. Can you lift the magnet slightly more so that the bat hovers by itself in mid-air, held up only by the invisible power of magnetism?

INDEX

accelerators 41, 60
aircraft 5
alloys 18
alternating current (AC) 47
Ampère, André Marie 37
amplifier 5, 54-5
Amundsen, Roald 29
Arctic tern 34
astronauts 31
atoms 7
attraction force 6, 12-19
Aurora Australis 31
Aurora Borealis 31
autopilot 5

bar magnet 17, 36
battery 40, 45
Bell, Alexander Graham 48
bismuth 21
blood 12
butterfly, migration 27, 35

can-opener 21, 46
cassette-player 4, 45-6, 52
cassette tape 50-1
collider 41
commutator 44
compact disk (CD) 45-6,
  51, 56-7
compass 5, 10-11, 17, 24,
  26-7, 32
  making 26-7
computer 4, 46, 56-7
  magnetic disk (MD) 20,
    50, 56-7

monitor 41, 56
  printer 41
  read-write head 56-7

diamagnetism 21
digital audio tape
  (DAT) 50
direct current (DC) 47
domains 7
dynamo 37, 44-5, 48

Earth's magnetism 24-6,
  28-30, 34-5
electricity 7, 36-41
electric motor 4, 20, 36-7,
  44-7, 60
electromagnet 7, 36-7,
  52-3
  future development
    60-1
  making 38-9
electromagnetic induction
  37, 44, 48, 55
electromagnetism (EM)
  36-44
EM Olympics 42-3
electron gun 41

Faraday, Michael 16, 37,
  44-5
Fender 55
ferro-magnetism 21
field
  electric 7
  electromagnetic 36-7
  magnetic 7, 16-17, 24
fish, migration 34-5
fishing, magnetic 22-3
Formula 1 58-9
fridge magnets 4, 15

generator 44-5, 48, 61
Gibson 55
Global Positioning System
  (GPS) 26
gold 21
gravity 24
guitar, electric 5, 48, 54-5

headphones 52-3
Henry, Joseph 37, 45
history of magnets 10-11
horseshoe magnet 6, 8,
  17, 36
inventions 62
iron 6-7, 12, 21
iron filings 16, 36
iron-alnico 53

Jupiter 31

keyboard instruments,
  electric 55

laser 51, 56-7
lead 21
lift 47
lines of magnetic force
  10, 16
lodestone 10-11
loudspeaker 48-9, 52-3

machinery 36-7, 40-1
Magnesia 11
magnetic disk (MD) 20,
  50, 56-7
magnetic levitation 15
magnetic resource imager
  (MRI) 40
magnetic reversal 29
magnetism 6
  destroying 9
  transferred 6
magnetite 10
magnetosphere 30
making a magnet 6, 8-9
maps 32-3
Mercury 31
metal detector 40
microphone 48-9
microwave oven 46
migration, birds and
  animals 34-5
motor vehicles 46-7

nano-machinery 47
navigation 5, 10-11, 26-7

birds and animals 34-5
satellite 5, 26
Northern Lights 31
north pole 14-16
  Geographic 28-9
  Magnetic 11, 15, 24-5,
    28-9, 32

Oersted, Hans Christian 37

palladium 21
paper-clip chain 6
para-magnetism 21
particle accelerator 41
Peary, Robert 29
permanent magnet 7, 20,
  36, 44, 53
pick-up 49, 55
Pixii, Hippolyte 45
planets 31
plasma power 60
platinum 21
poles 7, 10, 14-15
  Earth's 11, 15, 24-5, 28-9
  north 14-16
  south 14-16
Poulsen, Valdemar 51
power station 4, 44
  future developments 60-1
  plasma power 60

radio 4, 49
read-write head 56-7
record, vinyl 49, 51
recording sound 50-3
recycling metals 40, 61
reel-to-reel tape 50-1
repulsion force 14-16
Rickenbacker, Adolph 55
ring magnet 16
rocks, magnetic 10-11, 29
Ross, James 11

salvage equipment 22
samarium-cobalt 53
satellite 5, 26, 61
  launcher 61
  navigation 5, 26

Saturn 31
scanner, medical 40, 60
Scott, Robert Falcon 29
screwdriver 21, 47
seeing magnetism 16-17
shape 6-7, 15, 17
silver 21
size 6-7, 18
soft magnet 53
solar wind 30
solenoid 37
sound and magnetism
  48-55
  recording sound 50-1
Southern Lights 31
south pole 14-16
  Geographic 28-9
  Magnetic 15, 24-5, 28-9
Space 30-1, 61
  exploration 30-1, 61
speedometer 4
spontaneous permanent
  magnetism 36
steel 6, 8, 13, 18
storage media 50-1, 56-7
storm, magnetic 25
strength, testing 18-19
Sturgeon, William 38
switch 39-40, 42-3
synthesizer 55

tape, magnetic 50-3
tape recorder 50-3
telephone 48, 52
television 41
testing a magnet 9
tools, electric 4, 47
toys 37, 46
trains 5, 45, 47
transformer 37, 44
tricks with magnets 62-3
tweeter 53

Van Allen belts 30
video tape 50-1

weather 25
woofer 53

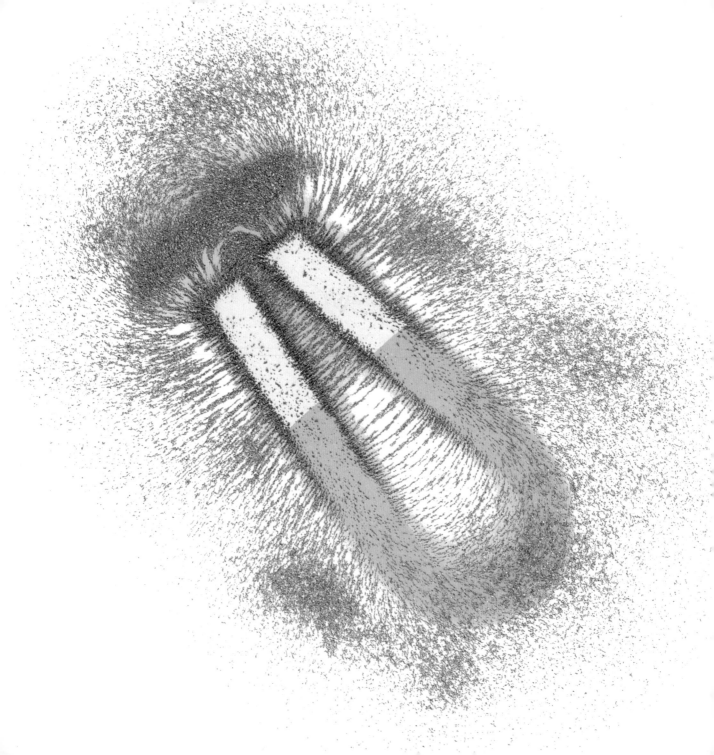